IRIS BARRY
POEMS

PUBLIC DOMAIN POETS

Editor: Dick Whyte   —: No. VIII :—   August 2022

IRIS BARRY (**1895-1969**) was born in Birmingham, England, and studied at the Ursulines convent in Belgium. Barry began writing and publishing poetry as early as 1914, already in the 'free verse' style. Ezra Pound read her work in *Poetry* in 1916, and offered to publish some of her poems, and in 1917 she moved to London to study with Pound. Once there Barry attended Imagist gatherings – attended by H.D., Richard Aldington, T.S. Elliot (et al.) – and regularly published poetry between 1916 and 1924. She also wrote a novel, *Splashing into Society*, in 1923, and started writing film criticism for *The Spectator* and *The Daily Mail* around the same time. After 1924 Barry stopped publishing poetry to focus on film criticism, co-founding the Film Society of London with Ivor Montagu in 1925, and writing one of the early classics of English-language film theory, *Let's Go To The Movies*, in 1926. Barry relocated to America in 1930, established the film department at the newly opened Museum of Modern Art in New York, and worked as a book reviewer for the *New York Times*.

'Cauchemar', 'Nightfall', 'Ocean', & 'Flirtation' (*Poetry & Drama*, Dec. 1914); 'The Daughter' (*Others: A Magazine of the New Verse*, July 1916); 'The Fledgling', 'Impression I', 'Study', 'Domestic', 'Double', 'Town Mouse', 'Impression II', & 'Enough Has Been Said Of Light' (*Poetry*, July 1916); 'His Girl', 'Widow', 'At the Hotel', 'At the Ministry', 'Towards the End', & 'The Black Fowl' (*The Little Review*, Aug. 1917); 'Mutual Recriminations' (*The Egoist*, Oct. 1917) & 'To My Head Clerk' (March 1918); 'Going to Work' & 'July 26th' (*The Apple*, Jan. 1920); 'Lovers' Meeting' (*The Chapbook*, March 1921); 'Shadow Songs' (*Poetry*, Sep. 1922); 'Love & Pride' (*The Chapbook*, June 1923); 'Lost' (*The Spectator*, Sep. 1924). 'Sub-Title' excerpted from Barry's book on cinema, *Let's Go To The Movies* (Chatto & Windus, 1926).

Cover: E. McKnight Kauffer – 'Decoration' & Jacob Kramer – 'Day of Atonement' (*The Chapbook*, 1923-24). Inside: Théophile Steinlen – 'Cat', Rupert Lee – 'Cats', Edgar Tytgat – 'Wash Drawing [seated woman]', Keith Baynes – 'Bare Trees'; & assorted ornaments (*The Apple*, 1920-21); Ethelbert White – 'Cover/Title Page', Andre Derain – 'Wood Engraving', & assorted ornaments by Terence Prentis, E.M. Kauffer, etc. (*The Chapbook*, 1922-25).

This collection ©2022. All individual poems, illustrations, and ornaments belong to the 'public domain', unless otherwise noted, and may be freely copied and/or distributed. Some elements of the originals may have been marginally edited, for clarity and consistency.

PUBLIC DOMAIN PRESS
Aotearoa / New Zealand
ISBN: 978-1-99-117760-5 (print) • 978-1-99-117761-2 (kindle)
978-1-99-117762-9 (pdf)

IRIS BARRY
IMPRESSIONS & STUDIES

POEMS

1914-1924

Sub-Title

The making of sub-titles might well be held to be a new form of literary style. The sub-title must be crystalline, packed with meaning, allusive, condensed—a work of art and elegance and simplicity, in fact. I think the *vers-librists* would make good title writers : they write fresh active pictorial phrases, they avoid redundancies, elaborations, clichés. Producers in America will have no trouble in discovering the best people in this school of poetry and in harnessing them. I myself have taken past exercise in *vers libre*, and for fear of seeming artful or impertinent, I frankly offer myself as an apprentice sub-titler for a period of six months to any film company that cares to have me. Brevity would be my motto and eloquence (not flowery eloquence but the small sweet voice) my ambition.

IRIS BARRY

POEMS

CAUCHEMAR

WAKED suddenly, and sitting upright, breathless
In that black deep of night when time is not,
Heart stopped, and throat clutched by a ghoulish fear
Was one, striving in anguish to recall
Some deed, some little deed of good once done,
Some deed to shame with light the nameless fear,
And strove in vain.

NIGHTFALL

I.

AT night my mother sits uncorseted
And with tired gestures combs her long hair.
Her head shines in the gaslight,
And she yawns, dropping many hair-pins
    as she goes upstairs.

II.
A clock ticks clearly in the very silent kitchen.
The old man coughs, and rising,
Going to the hearth, spits in the ashes.

III.
Where my visitor sat, little ends of silk litter the floor.
I like to remember that she has been in my room to-day.

OCEAN

TANGLE of seaweed, shut in my lover's book,
You are forgotten. But when I, curious,
Taste you, my tongue's tip cautiously trying
Finds you are salt. Quickly the great sea
Opens before me. I see my lover
Blown with the sea-breeze, bending to take you,
I see my lover pause before turning,
You in her fingers, blown with the sea-breeze,
Watch the sea heaving, feel all its vastness,
Know it estranges.

Tangle of seaweed,
Where did her thought fly? Thought in its vastness
Often estranges. Tangle of seaweed
Salt to my tongue's touch, shut between pages,
We are forgotten.

FLIRTATION

BEING in the country, a Colin made love to me
And we sat together on a great fallen tree at sunset.
But the trunk being slippery,
        a sudden movement to touch me
Made him lose balance, and falling backwards,
        pull me with him.
So that we got up vexed and embarrassed,
And quickly went home without further thought
        of lovemaking.

THE DAUGHTER

She had harbored heaped grudges
(But deep, for the hid money's sake)
Many years.
And now the body
Dried, and sore, continually bedridden,
Lies at last in the coffin:
And the cat
(Ever loathsome to the deceased)
Creeps in there and sleeps,
Sleeps curled by the stockinged feet with long nails.
The daughter discovering this, to her distraught
    mind
Retaliation seems possible,
And very quickly
Drives in the screws,
Working swiftly—
When finished, laughing.

All night
The yowling of the cat,
The spotted cat,
Continues,
And the unrest of all carrion
As also the laughter.

At intervals
The cat's efforts for escape
Are renewed, becoming feebler,
So the laughter.

But when the neighbors—
Coming to nail up the box
And assisting, interfere—
Arrive (long after dawn)
All but the unrest of all carrion
Has ceased.

THE FLEDGLING

The fire is nearly out,
The lamp is nearly out.
The room is untidy after the long day.
I am here, unhappy,
Longing to leave the hearth,
Longing to escape from the home.
The others are asleep,
But I am here, unhappy.
The fire is nearly out,
The lamp is nearly out.

IMPRESSION

The orchards are white again . . .
There was one I knew
Whose body was white as they: fairer.

Alas! that we drifted apart
Faster than pear-petals fall to the ground!

STUDY

Oh carrot cat, slinking over the snow,
Your skin is blue, where the bitter wind ruffles your fur.
Can you not find one shivering sparrow
    in all this white world?

DOMESTIC

Sometimes,
Having read
By the fireside
Through a long evening,
I look up.
The old people
Apathetically
Are sitting,
The dim eyes gazing
In the past
That seems so good.
And then pity
Dews all my sight.
For old age
Is the guerdon,
The only laurels,
Of their life.
And mine, uncrowned,
So far away,
I cannot cry
"Hail!"

DOUBLE

Through the day, meekly,
I am my mother's child.
Through the night riotously
I ride great horses.

In ranks we gallop, gallop,
Thundering on
Through the night
With the wind.

But in the pale day I sit, quiet.

TOWN-MOUSE

These things for today:
The threat of rain,
And great hasting clouds;
Wet soil's scent;
Fine cobwebs on the heather;
Keen air!
Even a park of green lawns,
Bare boughs and brown sparrows!
Oh, for no roof overhead
And full lungs!

These things for today.

IMPRESSION

   At night
Neither joy, ambition, love nor want
In my heart.
But the leaves called
And the earth called,
And there was only waiting
Against the coming of rain,
And the whipping of hair
About my head.

ENOUGH HAS BEEN SAID OF SUNSET

I

Light—imperceptible as
One thin veil drawn across blackness:
Is it dawn? . . .
Comes the twitter-whistle of sleepy birds
Crescendo . . .
Now bright grayness creeping
Drowns the dark; and waves of sea-wind
Rock the thin leaves . . .
A door bangs;
    sharp barks from dogs released, scampering.
After some silence, footsteps.
And the rising bustle of people
Roused by the day-break.

II

Mysterious; threatening:
Dawn over housetops silhouetted
Like crenelated battlements
Against light of a stage scene.

His Girl

The bigger boys, gathered round the gates in the dusk,
Watch her walk away with their teacher.
They stop shouting, somewhat astonished
That she should wait for him in the cold.
They do not see very much in him themselves
And stare, commiserating the stupidity of woman.

Widow

Monica may well modulate her voice
And pose as a charming and sympathetic person.
Everyone knows she has had two husbands
And driven both to a lasting great distance.

At the Hotel

While at table
Or chatting conventionally in the drawing-room
She eyes him.
They are seen together everywhere
Husband and wife.
Nothing but her vigilance binds them.
Her smoothness sickens him:
She is not even successful.
She may keep his body to her bed—
It is easier than a scene and remonstrances.

Towards dawn he turns, smiling,
Dreaming of a girl on the hotel-staff.
(Already he has trifled with her in his heart).

At the Ministry
September 1916

Having received the last volume of a certain poet
I look out of the office window—
Coloured shirts: green, blue, red, grey:
Men in coloured shirts moving
      heavy things with deliberation
Out there in the sun.

The junior typist cries ecstatically
On seeing the costly photogravure of the author,
Clasping her hands and flushing.
But I sit and look out
      at the irregular wandering shirts,
  At the men unloading projectiles
  And storing them in the dark sheds.

Towards the End

Others might find inspiration and wide content
In this mellow kitchen,
      the beams and washed walls,
Flagged floor lit by the log-glow:
But the beetles and mice appreciate it more than I.
And my Mother is bored to death,
(She keeps putting records on the gramaphone)
Even grandfather eating his supper
      by the jumping light from the hearth
Hardly seems to enjoy his food.
Very patriarchal-benign he looks.

      Somehow his shadow on the wall
          awes me in its grandeur
As though he might not be here long,
And the beetles and mice
      come into their own very shortly.

MUTUAL RECRIMINATIONS

NOW you have cleared away the boughs
   And long grass
   And can look into the pool
Which is me,
You say you are disappointed !
You " thought white or yellow lilies
Floated there " !

A more finished lover would have known
They had vanished.

TO MY HEAD CLERK

DO you know
   What lies under the hedgerow grass-stalks ?
   Have you seen
Where the frogs close their bronze eyes ?
   Has the plover
Screamed you a field away from her four eggs ?

   Or has it been always thus
   With ledgers and a buzz of nothings ?

The Black Fowl

Black fowl, perching,
I have seen nothing
    more beautiful than your plumes.
It should be pleasant to nestle
    luxuriously in that rich black.
But there is no joy
    in the winking eye that watches me
As you stand there perching.

GOING TO WORK
Prostrate before the surging waves,
The successive waves of the racing wind,
Bow the shining spears
   Of winter grass
   In the grimed gardens.

    Overhead
Leers the yolk-red sun
    Angry
In the leaden sky
Like a fierce lantern.
And the work-bound puppets pulled unpityingly
    By the strings of circumstance
      Jostle me by.

Morning : always the same street, same passers,
Always the same pulse in my mind,
    Alternately hope and fear.
Children reluctantly chewing bread and jam
    Scamper to school,
Not gazing back on their homes,
    Not making plans.

    Morning again.

JULY 26th

Summer, you darling, at last!
Wherever have you been all this time?
Rain has drenched everything, the mornings and evenings
Blown so cold while you dawdled,
Why have you stayed out of town so long?
The sweat stands wet and round on the flower-sellers'
    faces
(They have covered their baskets of roses
With blue cabbage-leaves
Placing them where shopblinds throw a small shadow)
And some sprinkle water
Out of sea-coloured bottles.
You can smell wet dust and flowers,
While girls in frivolous dresses
Festoon like butterflies about the hot streets.

Summer, you darling,
You have flung blue sky
Like a chiffon scarf over the town!

Lovers' Meeting

I AM irretrievably lost :
Bright agate her eyes,
And a chasm her heart
Where a few dead men
Worm-wriggle, corruption-tossed.
Oh, without warning bell, smiling at men,
Passes this death-cart,
My . . . .

I am irretrievably lost,
And will no more minimise
What every nodding neighbour knows,
But go shouting mad
For love in a dark wood.
Yet no wolf would
Nor no raven tear
Nor harm me, well aware
There runs such poison through my blood
As ate up Waldemar invisibly.
So I am dead of her dark mesmery
Though seeming whole, yet long dead of her beauty,
An irremediably unburied ghost,

Till one day, while I am wandering in the wood
(For even she
Can't stand the beauty of spring for ever)
I think she will cover her face,
And fall and whimper for me : " Oh, my good,
My most brave lover ! "
Anguish and death together
Will take her.
(She shall not brave the beauty of spring forever,
Leaves crashing in green chords
On myriad black boughs :

Cherry-trees flinging fountains heavenwards,
To the blue heaven, oh, blue heaven, then—
Dissolving beauty,
Dissolving the evil that she gave to men.)

Then I shall shiver from a living darkness
And dissolve and fall to a sudden mess,
Dripping down.
(Will she say, " Oh my good,
My most brave lover, to thy feet,
Thy manifold and soft white formless feet
I come ? ")

Slow white worms shall toil
All glistening,
Shall crawl together, through soft soil,
A-writhe under the sweet cherry-flood :
Till so much smooth bare whiteness
Laced up in such a passion as ours then,
(Crawling, a-crawl my snake,
      my poison, soft white thing)
Shall blanch and kill these great trees in the wood.

SHADOW SONGS

LAMENTATION

Chrysanthemums and late roses
And the plane-leaf's fall—
All that is left us now.
Hoarsely the flower-girls cry,
Pale shake the street-lamp lights;
Chilled gusts come puffing by,
Sigh the poor year away.
All that is left us now
Regrets without perfume; dead thoughts;
Chrysanthemums, and late roses.

VIRGIN MOON

Having chattered out
The overbrimming of their light hearts,
When the old moon had traveled over the housetops
Far enough to dangle dancing shadows of leaves
Across their bed,
Veils of silence also were let down,
And they slept, virgin beside virgin.
The whisper of leaves outside the window
Filled the room
Long after the moon had trailed
Her net of shadow-boughs across their dreams
And was gone.

AN UNPOSTED LETTER

How bitter must the smile
Of the wise Future be
Behind her veil!
O letter of last year,
Can my hopes and aims,
    Like moons,
Have changed so?
Those dead desires,
Like shriveled fruits,
Hang, shamed,
On the bough of time.

NOCTURNE

The veil of light slipped
From the sky:
Only greyness.
And in the valley
One home light—
Not mine.

I most remember, then,
Shadows of boughs
Lattice-wise falling
On white walls
Of my home
Beneath the moon.

Love and Pride

RUBBING the steel flesh of a used heart
When the acid bites again
Proves hardening useless.
Formed like a bird,
  And fluttering like a great bird,
Wrathfully the spirit
Entered my room,
Filling it with soft wild sound,
Crying with sweet and incomprehensible sweetness.
The restless beating and crying
Attacking like aural anæsthetic
Reft self from body,
Floating it to some rare place,
Ever crying and beating wings,
Crashing and folding up sense:

Till a flute-voice, cloud-floating
    shadow-voice from brain, said :
" A pale frigid child
Places his crystal heart against thine."
That was the end and cause of vision.

Some walk now past the dwelling
Gazing up at the window
Till I, social, look out and nod.
All this while
The clear eye of a pale child
Watches my dreams,
And the wind blowing in at the window
Sees how I rub, polish, at the steel of my used heart
Where the acid bites again.

LOST.

When the boy knocked at our door, looking in,
We remember now that we spoke to him timidly,
Kept him waiting in the porch,
While we busied ourselves within over a fitting reception.

When we called him,
We found the porch empty.
Hop-vines and ivy trembled there,
A frame lacking its picture.
Nor can any tell us
Whether he ran along the road or the field-path.

This Space for Your Thoughts

Please handle with care.

www.ingramcontent.com/pod-product-compliance
Lightning Source LLC
Chambersburg PA
CBHW031947070426
42453CB00007BA/503